# THE BEST OF

# DADDY

D1350142

# THE BEST OF

# DADDY

## BY
## RUPERT FAWCETT

BOXTREE

First published 1996 and 1997 by Boxtree
an imprint of Macmillan Publishers Ltd
25 Eccleston Place, London SW1W 9NF
and Basingstoke

Associated companies throughout the world

ISBN 0 7522 1769 0

9  8  7  6  5  4  3  2  1

A CIP catalogue record for this book is available from the British Library.

Printed and bound in Great Britain by Redwood Books, Trowbridge, Wiltshire

Not being content with the huge success of his cartoon character, Fred, whose greeting cards continue to sell in millions, Rupert Fawcett has come up with another brilliant creation in DADDY.

THE BEST OF DADDY features the entire range of Daddy cartoons as previously published by Boxtree. With over 120 illustrations, it follows the trials and tribulations of the hapless Daddy as he struggles to come to terms with the realities of parenthood.

Rupert was born and brought up in West London where he still lives with his wife and (surprise, surprise) two small children.

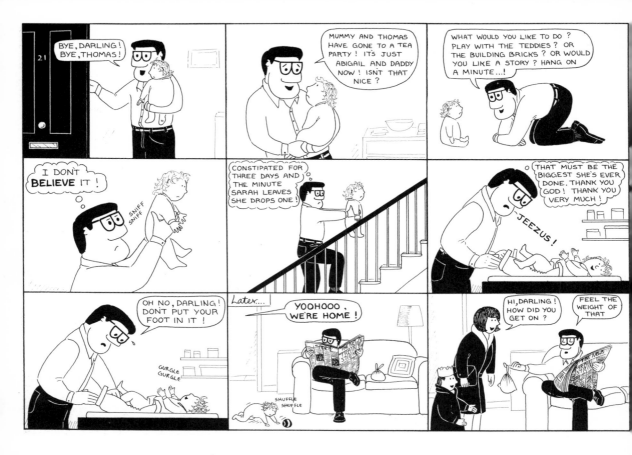

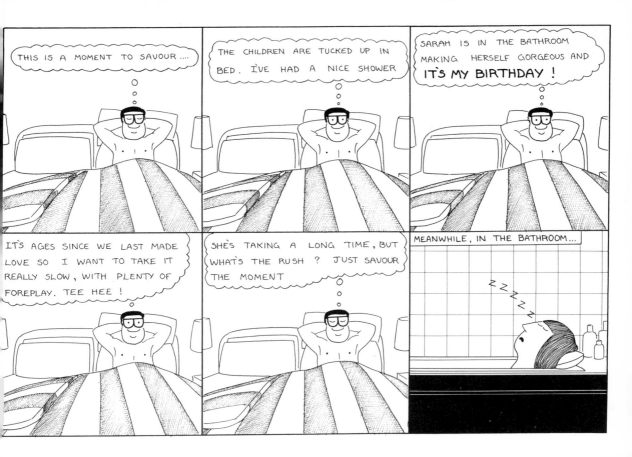

1.

2.

5.

6.

3.

4.

7.

8.

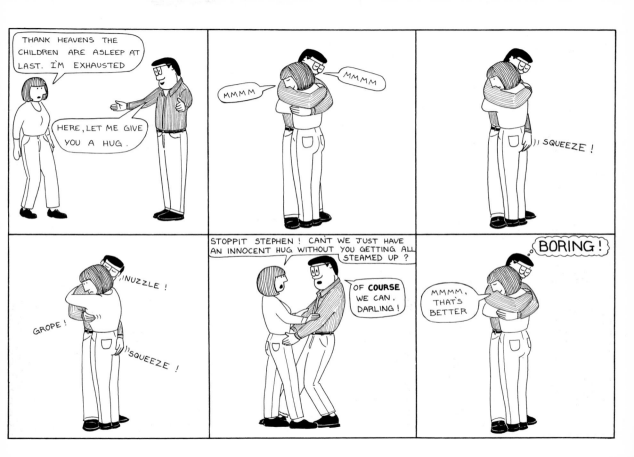

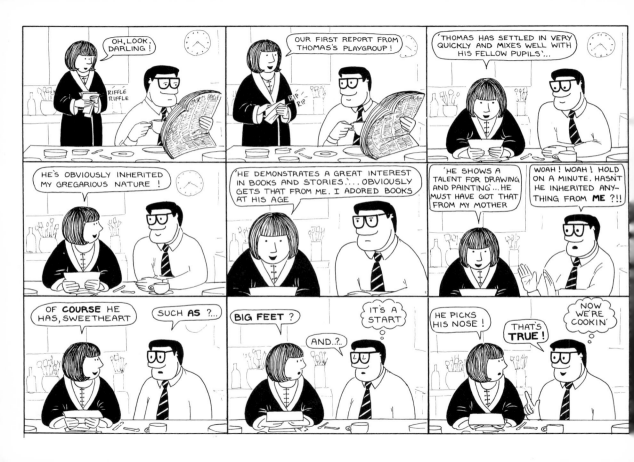

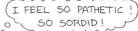

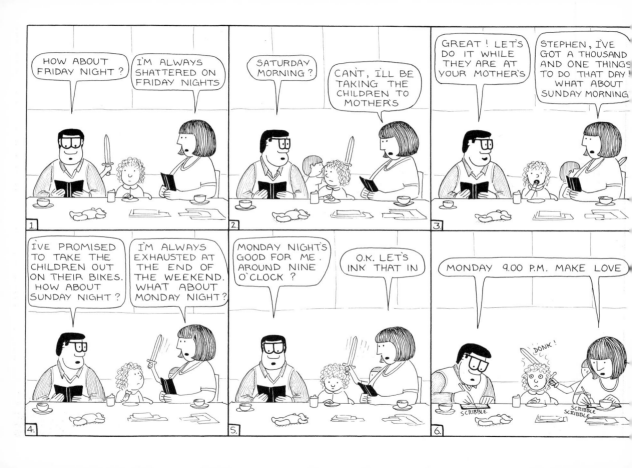

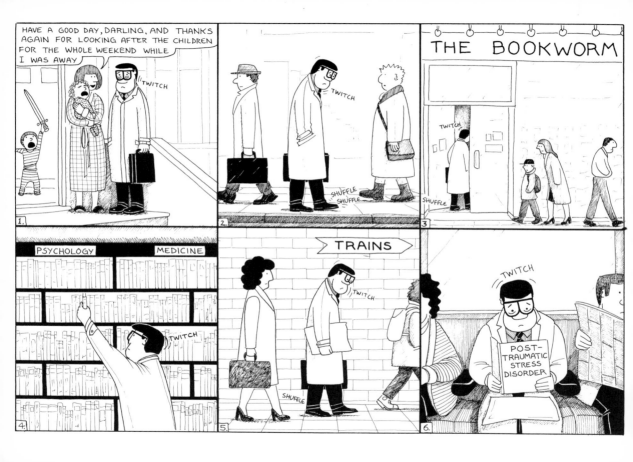

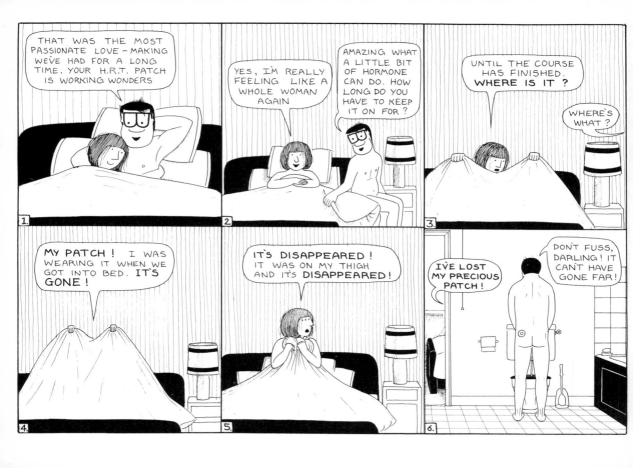

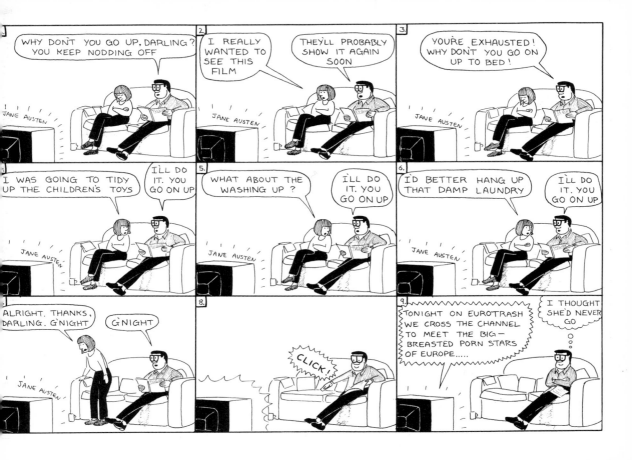

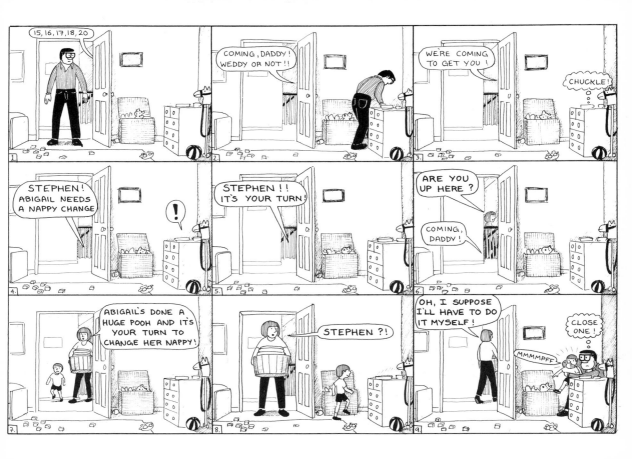

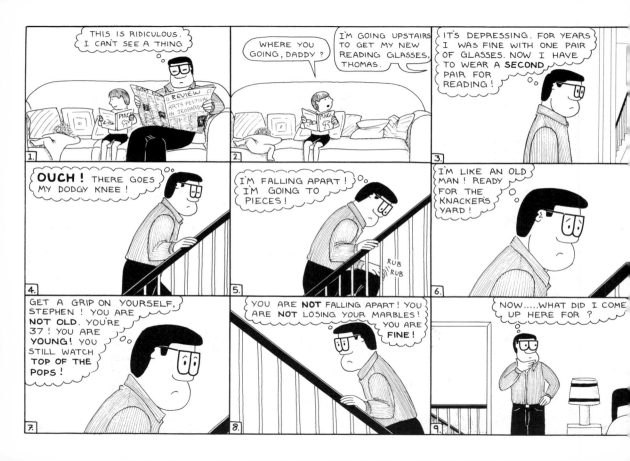